AMATL COMIX #1

MORE THAN MONEY

A Memoir by Claudia Dominguez

Afterword & Interview by Sam Cannon
Foreword by Frederick Luis Aldama

SAN DIEGO STATE UNIVERSITY PRESS

#amatlcomix

amatlcomix.sdsu.edu

More than Money: A Memoir by Claudia Dominguez is the first issue of Amatl Comix, an imprint published by San Diego State University Press.

San Diego State University Press publications may be purchased at discount for educational, business, or sales promotional use. For information write our Next Generation Publishing Initiative (NGPI), c/o SDSU PRESS, San Diego, California 92182-6020 or contact the press director, Dr. William A. Nericcio via email at bnericci@sdsu.edu.

sdsupress.sdsu.edu
facebook.com/sdsu.press
hype.sdsu.edu

amatlcomix.sdsu.edu
facebook.com/amatlcomix

Cover illustration by Claudia Dominguez
Cover and Book Design by Guillermo Nericcio García
for memogr@phics designcasa

ISBN-13: 978-1-938537-12-7
ISBN-10: 1-938537-12-2

FIRST EDITION

PRINTED IN THE UNITED STATES OF AMERICA

TABLE OF CONTENTS

The Birth of Amatl Comix

William Anthony Nericcio

I t is not often that publishers and directors of presses step from out of the shadows to directly address their readership. But this is not a common time—not at all a moment to be silent. Like some latter-day incarnation of Oscar Zoroaster Phadrig Isaac Norman Henkle Emmannuel Ambroise Diggs, aka, the Wizard of Oz, that charming snake-oil salesman in L. Frank Baum's novel and Victor Fleming's movie (who lurked surreptitiously behind the curtains before being revealed), I emerge here before you, a press director and professor, but *also* as someone totally nuts about comics.

Truth be told, I never would have succeeded in the bizarre odyssey that brought me to the peculiar walls of the Ivory Tower without comics. After all, it was back in the 1960s at my Grandmother Ana Juarez di Nericcio's house, (619 Mier Street; Laredo, Texas), and with my stalwart sidekick and best friend at my side, my sister Josie Nericcio, that I learned to read (and to read and see with and through comics).

At first it was Warren Kremer's *Richie Rich,* Sgt. George Baker's *Sad Sack* and Dan De Carlo's *Betty and Veronica,* that opened the door, or, even, blasted my optical synapses with their visual cacophony of word and image.[1]

---

[1] Warren Kremer, *Warren Kremer Richie Rich Dollars & Cents #37 Cover 1970* Artist: Warren Kremer (Penciller) http://www.comicartfans.com/GalleryPiece.asp?Piece=1432095, accessed 7 February 2018; George Baker, *Sad Sack,* from https://www.mycomicshop.com/search?TID=197591, accessed 7 February 2018; Dan DeCarlo, from Rick Diehl's "... Home to Every Cool Thing in the Universe," "A classic Dan DeCarlo splash panel, *Archie Comics: Betty & Veronica* #69." http://studdblog.blogspot.com/2011/06/classic-dan-decarlo-splash-panel.html, accessed 7 February 2018.

From there I moved on to bigger, better, more challenging graphic narratives like those of Jim Aparo's *Batman*, Harvey Kurtzman and Will Elder's *Mad* comic parodies, and Rius's Mexy Marxist ramblings.[2]

After finishing my Comparative Literature degree in 20th century Latin American literature at Cornell University, I went on to the fame and fortune of being a West Coast-based English Professor at SDSU. There, I met the former publisher/director of SDSU Press, Dr. Harry Polkinhorn (who is now a practicing shrink, but that's another story). Whilst dabbling in the arcane arts of English professory, Harry let me work at SDSU Press as a contributing editor, where I also snuck in, behind the scenes, working on the side as a book designer (I had been a frustrated cartoonist and would-be comic book artist my entire life, the sketch opposite giving you a sense of "my range" (and proof in the pudding that I chose the right profession!).

Flash forward many years later and I am the director of SDSU Press. I look over my shoulder and I see that my book-factory-of-a-friend, the prolific *Fede* Aldama (aka Dr. Frederick Luis Aldama, Distinguished Professor, the Ohio State University) is starting up a line of comics called *Latinografix* with the Ohio State University Press. Fueled with envy and ambition, it occurs to me that San Diego, poised on the tip of the West Coast and home to

[2] Jim Aparo panel from Ross Burlingame's "Top Ten Batman Artists of All Time," http://comicbook.com/blog/2012/04/11/top-ten-batman-artists-of-all-time/, Accessed 7 February 2018; Harvey Kurtzman and Will Elder, "Starchie" *Mad Magazine #12* (1954), from Four Color Shadows, http://fourcolorshadows.blogspot.com/2013/11/starchie-harvey-kurtzmanwill-elder-1954.html, accessed 3 March 2018; Rius, Eduardo del Río, *Marx para principiantes* (Ediciones de cultura popular, 1972) via https://www.abebooks.com/servlet/BookDetailsPL?bi=21270898220, Accessed 3 March 2018.

the world-famous Comic-Con conventions, just might be the place to host a new comics publishing venture—and *voilà!* The rest is history, as you hold the first issue in your hands.

About our name: Amatl Comix. The word *"Amatl"* is the Aztec (*Nahuatl*) word for the tree-bark-based paper onto which the pre-contact civilizations of central Mexico inscribed their earliest histories, narratives, myths, bookkeeping, etc.—these codices (as you can see here in a detail from the Codex Selden) reveal a culture immersed in the pictographic sharing of narrative information, and, in a way, reveal the Mexica to be the first practitioners of comic book storytelling in what will come to be called "North America."

Am I saying the Mexica dug comics? In a way, yes. But I am also suggesting that there is a long narrative tradition of telling stories here in the Americas that ties together worlds semantic with worlds semiotic, word and image together, fused, in flux, and reproducing in loud, living colors.

In other words, there's nothing new about Amatl Comix—if anything, we are a throwback publisher to a pre-Gutenberg mode of publishing that was tellingly modern and formidably contemporary centuries ago.

It is fitting that Claudia Dominguez's *More than Money* inaugurates the birth of Amatl Comix, now an imprint of San Diego State University Press. Her moving tale, a compelling and moving mélange of word and image coming from Mexico, works to reveal yet another hidden, unknown, saga from the history of the Americas in a decidedly adept, complex and 21st century manner.

See you in the funny pages,

Dr. William "Memo" Nericcio
Director, SDSU Press
Publisher, Amatl Comix

Latinx Graphic Memoir as Triumph of Love over Hate: A Foreword

Frederick Luis Aldama

We've been creating visual-verbal narratives since before the conquest of the Américas—and today more abundantly than ever. This is perhaps not so surprising. Our numbers are growing. Our practitioners of this narrative art are rapidly diversifying. And, with low-cost low-tech shaping devices, these creators use their resplendent visual-verbal storyworlds to reach into and radically transform all genres, experiences, and identities.

However shaped and expressed in all of its sensuous characteristics, visual-verbal storytelling arts are like carefully built houses but where the *bricoleur* uses as her prime matter all that come from the abundant universe of feelings, thoughts, knowledges, experiences, and guesses. . . all leading to a final outcome previously more or less clearly foreseen but very rarely attained in its most precise and pristine terms. As Claudia Dominguez's *More than Money: A Memoir* attests, the creating of a visual-verbal narrative is a disciplined activity performed with a result or aim in mind and concerned with specific materials and their transformations to create new realities and outlooks or innovative ways of looking at things. It springs from autobiographical experience as situated within the language, culture, history, socio-politics that inform Latinx hemispheric identities and subjectivities. Dominguez asks that we perceive, evaluate, analyze and enjoy this devastating moment in the life of her family—and that many of us Latinxs unfortunately relate to all too well—in all its emotional complexity: Latinx lives lived in fear.

As we travel through Claudia Dominguez's narrative we experience the unique ways that she chooses to *geometrize* her story. Dominguez's memoir gives idiosyncratic shape to space design, inking, lettering, balloon placement and size, perspective and geometric shaping. Dominguez's careful use of color wash shifts moods from light to dark, and all that comes in between; her figural reconstructions (the father's kidnapping imagined as him being scooped by a big net, for instance), make new our perception, emotions, and thoughts around this constant fear of tragic loss that many of our family members experience in their daily lives; and that we, also, feel from afar. And, unlike most mainstream representations of Latinxs in the Américas that depict us as only of European descent, Dominguez's palette celebrates us as mestizo. And while Dominguez chooses to use the traditional 6-panel layout sparingly, she does so to great kinetic effect, conveying the urgency and anxiety as it builds to the moment of exchanging money for family. She wakes our hearts and minds to the complex ways that Latinxs live as a hemispheric population connected through more than violence; her careful selection of everyday life rituals and cultural details that include *conversaciónes de sobremesa*, soccer, and religion. . . all become ways that connect us across borders. She invites us to find our way to and through singular or multiple languages, proximate and distant histories, as well as gender, sexuality, and class marked spaces. Dominguez chooses to convey behavior, action, and conflict in ways that affirm the expansive complexity of our identities and experiences despite (and resisting and pushing against) the constrains and socially handicapping conditions of fear we are being forced to live in our daily life today.

Hyperbole's Amatl Comics along with my Latinographix trade-press series with the Ohio State University Press have become much needed venues for our Latinx visual-verbal narrative artists. Sidelined by the titans of the mainstream publishing industry, high quality Latinx creations like *More than Money* urgently need publishers and editors committed to their production and distribution. It's a fact that while US Latinxs make up more than 18% of the population, in terms of representation in the marketplace we are reflected in less than 2% of cultural phenomena. Amatl and Latinographix seek to make a difference by providing our Latinx creators venues to create and share their visual-verbal stories in the ways that they choose.

It's a mind bogglingly extraordinary moment in the history of the Latinx visual-verbal narrative arts. As producers or as consumers, our numbers are growing steadily. And the creative imagination of our narrative-visual practitioners is penetrating all geographies, all social and historic settings, all human experiences, thereby reaching into and modifying all previous storyworlds and genres made possible by the new cultural and demographic circumstances. And, when the world increasingly seems to be barely holding itself together (and this increasingly out of fear), with *More than Money* Claudia Dominguez reminds us of the power of art—and above all else, art's capacity to represent love.

CHAPTER 1

The Kidnapping

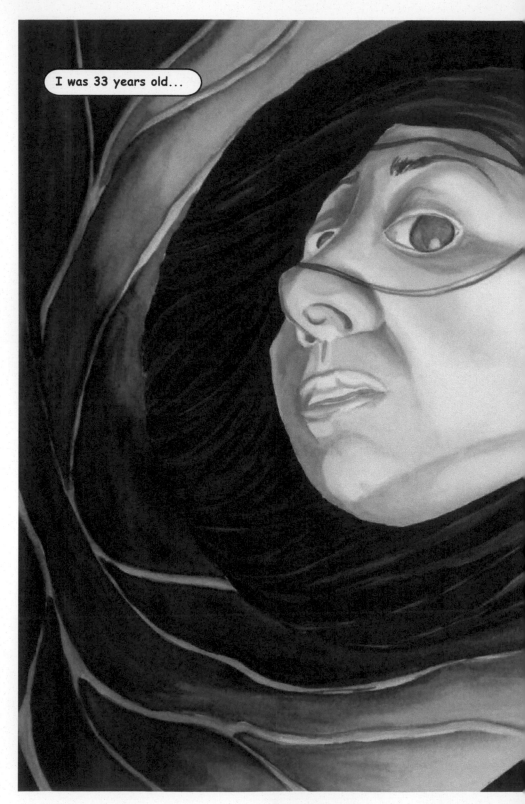

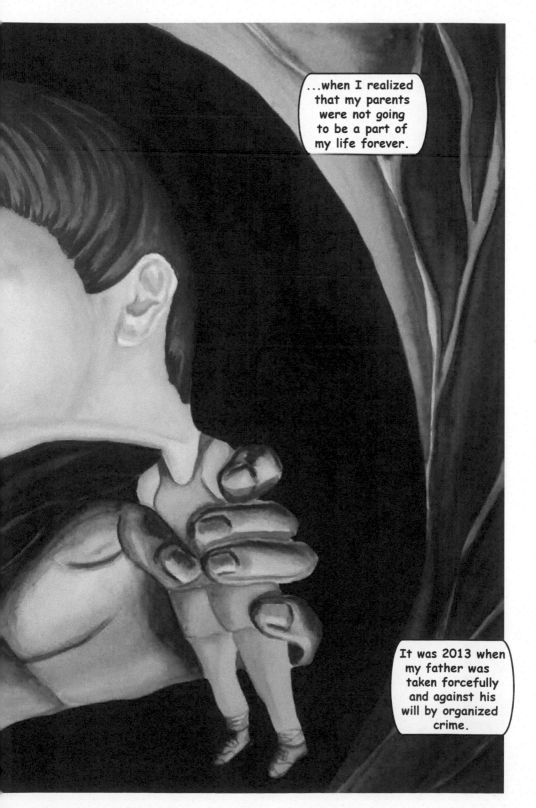

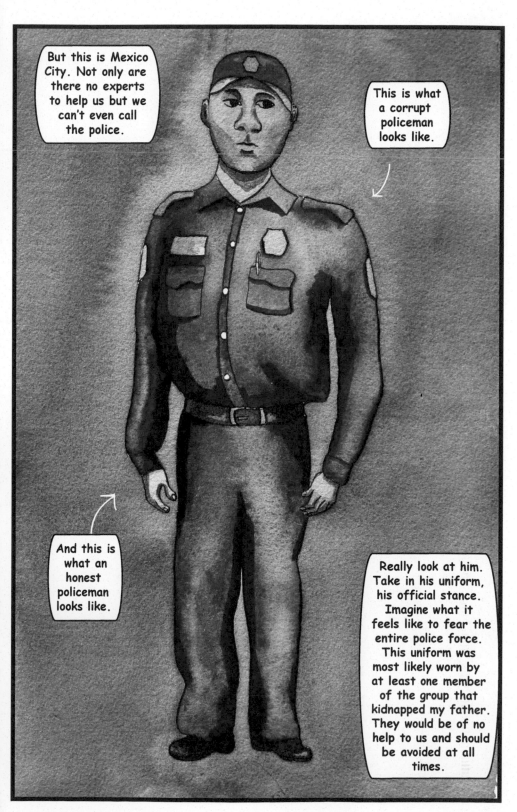

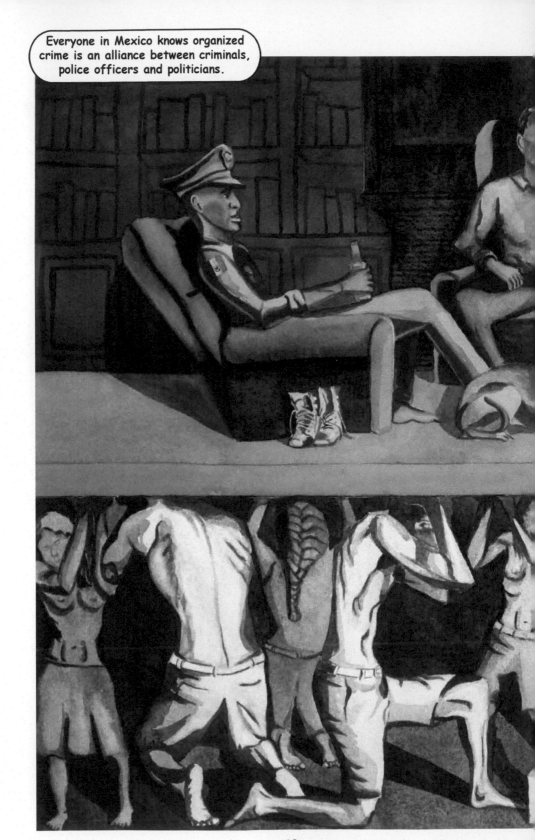

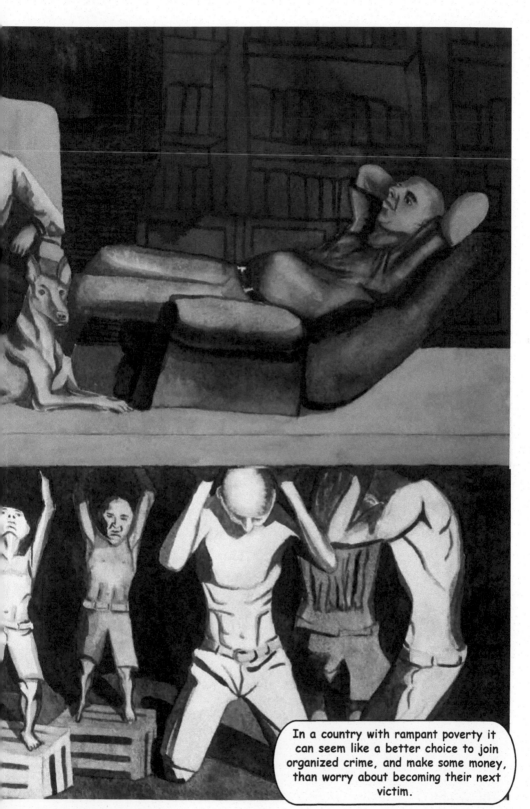

In a country with rampant poverty it can seem like a better choice to join organized crime, and make some money, than worry about becoming their next victim.

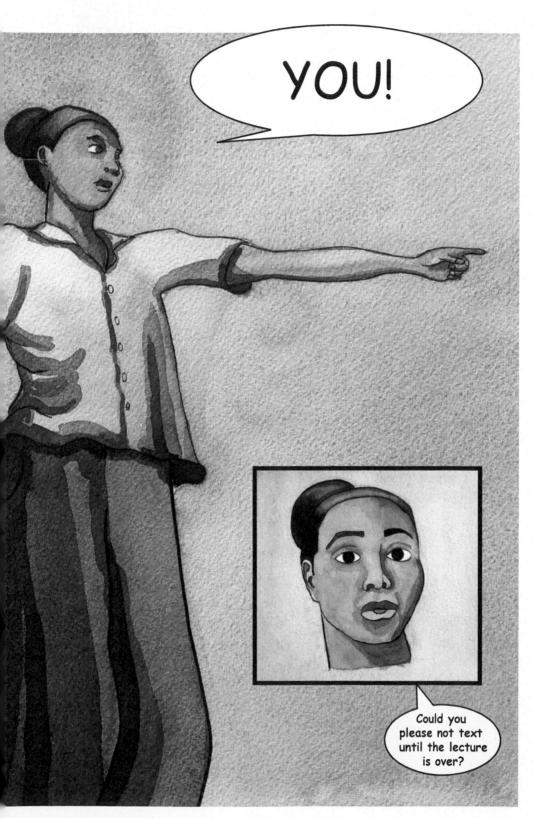

My husband and I had just moved to start our new teaching jobs.

We had recently been able to purchase a beautiful little house.

It is in this new neighborhood,

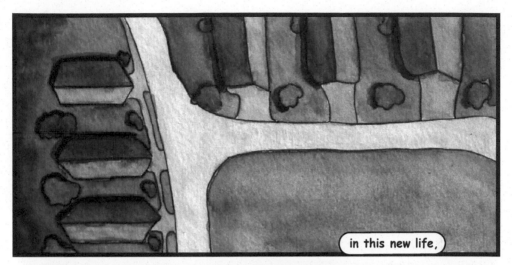

in this new life,

and in this new house that I sit paralyzed, waiting for any news from my family.

It's so good to finally hear from you sister!

We know he was taken at the campground but nothing else yet. I'm going to Mexico.

Mexico? You are not, uhm, afraid?

I am, but I'm going anyway. I'll call you when I know more.

I really hope I get to watch the world cup with him one more time.
I am Mexican, so I obviously root for Mexico in the world cup.
As an American citizen, I cheer for the American team as well.
10
They play with such passion!

We had celebrated the holidays as if we had all the time in the world to be together.

Following tradition, we had made tamales.

My dad and my niece had kneaded the dough for hours.

We knew it was ready when a small piece of it floated in a cup of water.

Vegetables and meats were cut.

Spices were prepared.

Banana leaves were roasted,

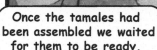

washed,

and cut.

All the ingredients were assembled in neat little bundles that were tightly wrapped and sealed. They were then carefully placed in a pot to be steamed.

Once the tamales had been assembled we waited for them to be ready.

We played games and drank wine as if we would be able to do this for the rest of our lives...

...until my mother announced with pride, that the tamales were ready.

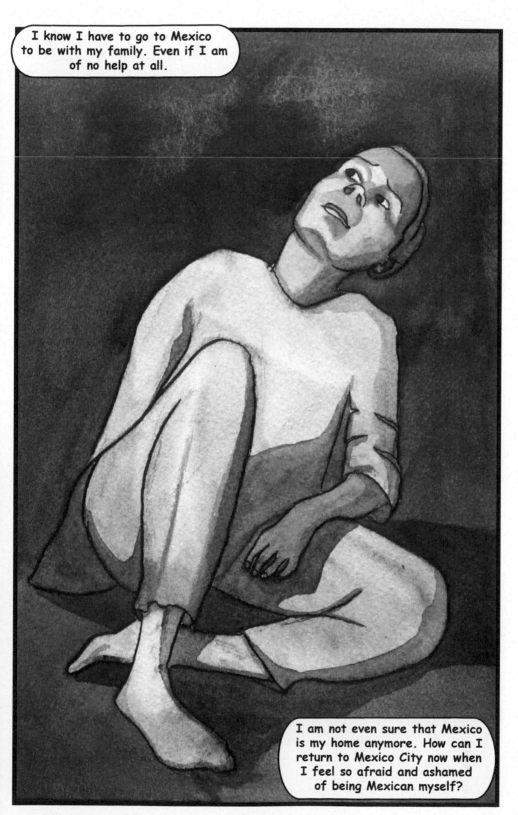

27

I used to spend my weekends riding the orange subway...

...from our home in the outskirts of the city to the downtown area.

On the weekend the subway was a colorful place full of surprises...

...like warm snacks,

live music,

and creative electronics salesmen.

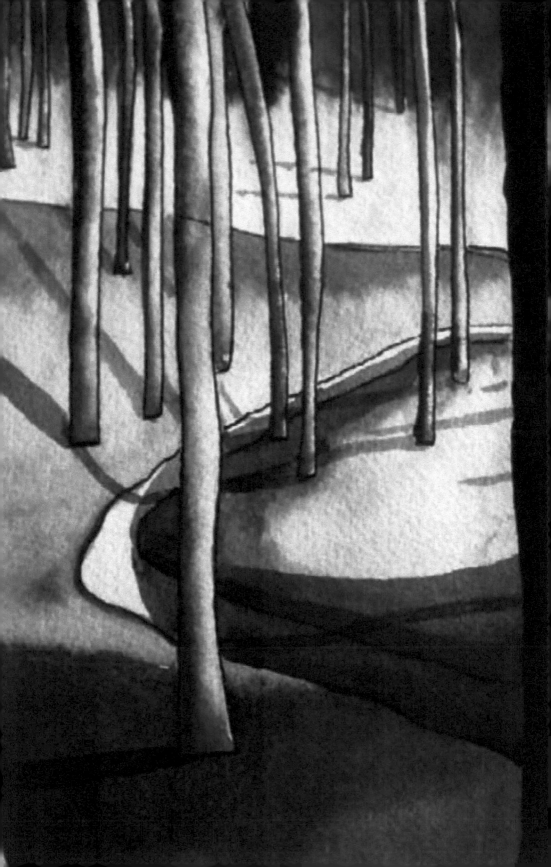

CHAPTER 2

Why Him?

I am grateful to be at the airport where I can be distracted from the worry about my father.

I am trying my best to keep my thoughts on the task at hand. I am trying to maintain a clear and helpful mind.

The least frightening thoughts are the most practical.

I can't allow myself to wonder about where he could be...

...or what shape he might be in.

I keep thinking: Why? Why him?

Kidnappings in Mexico have become disturbingly common.

So common that the media has coined the term "Express Kidnapping" for when someone is taken for less than 24 hours.

I had become oddly desensitized to these crimes and how they hurt the victim, the victim's family and society in general.

And I really hope I get to see my father again.

My sister told me that my father had been taken from the campground our family owns on the outskirts of Mexico City.

The campground was originally an empty lot that my father had hoped to convert into an RV facility...

...for Americans and Canadians to use while traveling south for the winter.

Soon after he bought it, it became clear that neither Canadians nor Americans were going to come.

My parents transformed it into a campground for schoolchildren in Mexico City.

They then organized activities around a pool,

a zip line,

and cooking.

On one of my visits to the campground my father told me that I was in for a treat. We were going to go on a moonwalk because of the full moon.

My sister is waiting for us.

Small yet tough, my sister has been my protector and guide for as long as I can remember.

I am ready to follow any instructions she might give me.

So now what?

How had the garden my mother used to water barefoot become too dangerous to stand in?

How had the porch where I had lazily petted my dog become too scary to sit on?

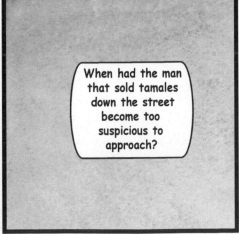

When had the man that sold tamales down the street become too suspicious to approach?

CHAPTER 3

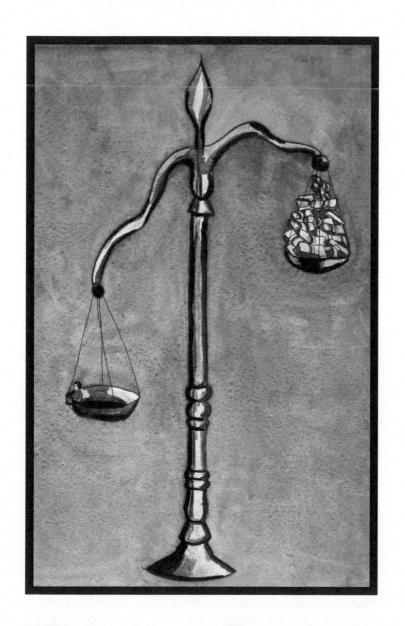

This is a Business Transaction

I can't help but be paranoid entering the hotel.

Even though this hotel will be our temporary refuge, my entire sense of safety is gone.

Worst of all, everything and everyone around me seems suspicious.

We have four rooms.

And to my delight...

...a secret knock

- knock, knock

We know it's you Claudia, just come in.

There is nothing to do but wait for the phone to ring.

Time passes slowly and uneasily.

We are afraid to answer the phone but terrified of not getting the call at all.

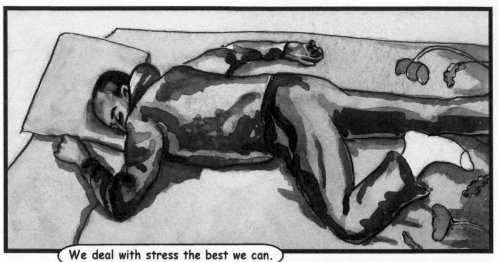

We deal with stress the best we can.

Some of us sleep,

long, long hours.

As much as we try to be kind, we also argue bitterly.

Finding ourselves upset over grievances we hadn't aired since childhood.

The fighting is unbearable and pointless.

Especially when our mother, on many mornings...

...wears her sweater inside out until one of us notices and fixes it.

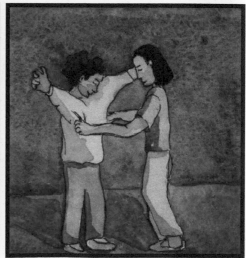

Even though we have a helpful advisor, I can't imagine what the ransom call will bring.

How do we assign a monetary value to my father's life?

I imagine my father's weight in his favorite Mexican sweet bread.

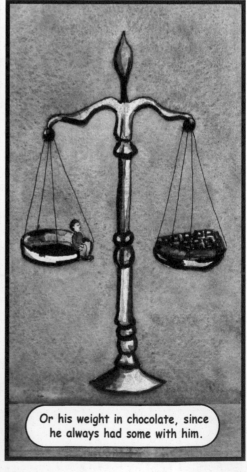

Or his weight in chocolate, since he always had some with him.

And yet we tally our accounts for the negotiation and reach out to friends and family to prepare for the worst.

Thank you for offering money, I will call you back if we need it.

We haven't recieved a ransom call yet but we are hopeful that we will get one soon.

All that
is left
is the
painful...

...empty...

...wait.

Until we hear
the phone ring.

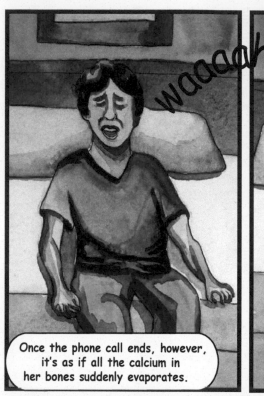

waaaah!

Once the phone call ends, however, it's as if all the calcium in her bones suddenly evaporates.

It's my job to surround her until she can find herself again.

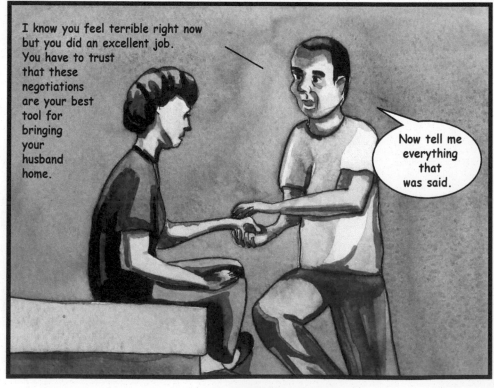

I know you feel terrible right now but you did an excellent job. You have to trust that these negotiations are your best tool for bringing your husband home.

Now tell me everything that was said.

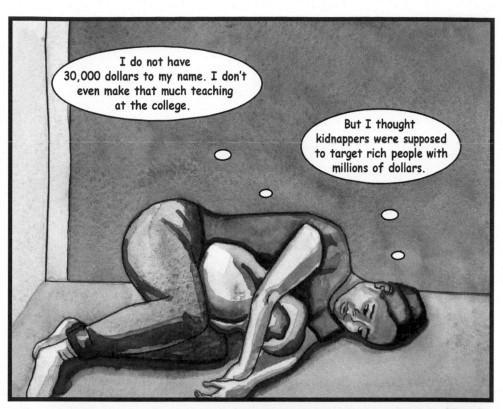

Is it true then that the very people that are in charge of preventing these crimes are the ones committing them?

Or is this simply a sign of how poor and desperate Mexico has become that people get kidnapped for any amount of money?

How American have I become that I think of 30,000 dollars as a house payment or a new car but not necessarily a life-changing sum.

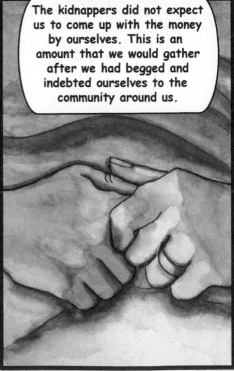

The kidnappers did not expect us to come up with the money by ourselves. This is an amount that we would gather after we had begged and indebted ourselves to the community around us.

Have my two homes - the U.S. and Mexico - always had such disparities in income and law enforcement? Is this violence and desperation in Mexico new?

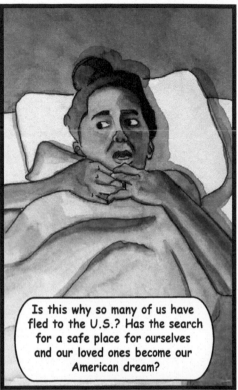

Is this why so many of us have fled to the U.S.? Has the search for a safe place for ourselves and our loved ones become our American dream?

And how am I ever going to find the peace to sleep and the patience to wait for tomorrow's phone call?

At approximately 3:30 pm we nervously gather around the phone.

Every time we wait for the call, I fear that the phone will never ring and that the kidnappers will not contact us.

Our advisor guesses that the kidnappers call at 4:00 pm because this marks the end of a work shift...

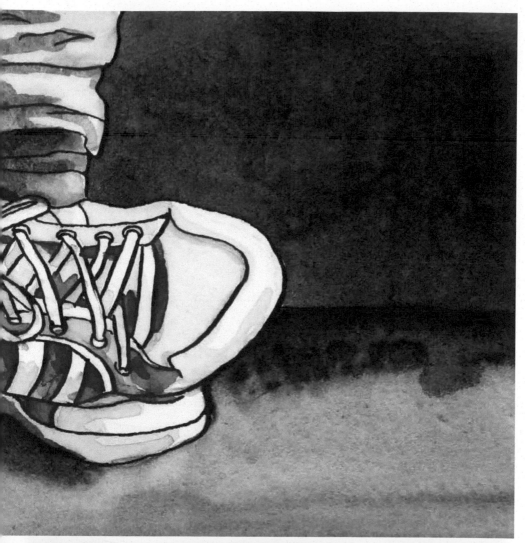

...as if negotiating for a ransom were a casual side job performed after a full day of policing or selling goods at the market.

I know it is painful to think of your father in the hands of these people but...

..this is the fastest and safest way to bring him home.

If you had given the kidnappers one million pesos, they would've turned around and asked for more.

And we would be back at the beginning of the negotiations. This is progress.

CHAPTER 4

The Ransom

Between phone calls I struggle to control the fear that threatens to paralyze me. I don't leave the hotel often but for the rare visit to a nearby supermarket.

The disconcerting explosion of colors and smells puts me on guard. I'm wary of the noise and suspicious of all people.

I ball my hands into fists, feeling that everyone here could be a threat to me and mine.

We go to several different banks...

...until all of our bills are 20s and 50s

Once all the bills are divided, we drop them onto a bed. My sister-in-law and I must count and package the bills appropriately.

I've never handled this much cash in my life and I can't help but contemplate the horror of what people do to accumulate these pieces of paper. Looking at it on the bed changes my relationship to money instantly and irrevocably.

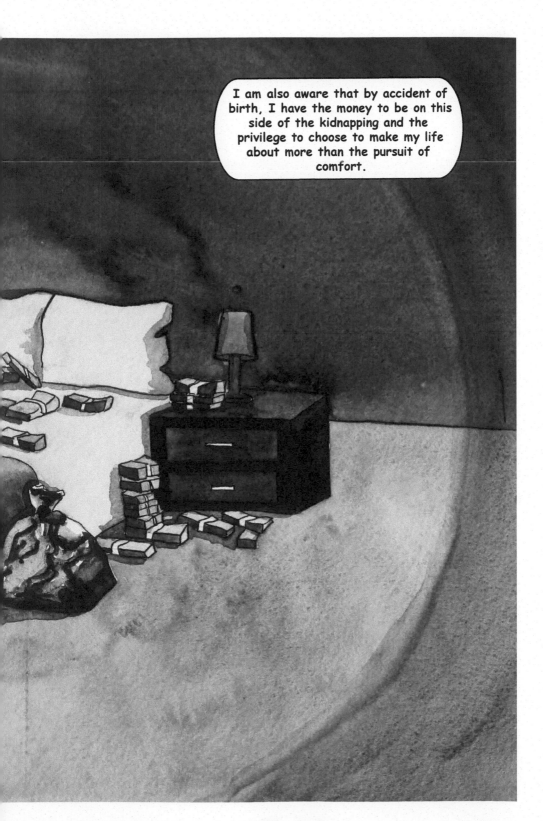

We count the money four times, passing the bundles to each other to double-check the amount. When we finish, we count it four more times because there can be no mistakes.

My mother had spoken to me about forgiveness, about how hating the kidnappers wasn't good for anyone. I couldn't agree with her and I had dismissed the advice as nonsense, completely beyond my ability to empathize.

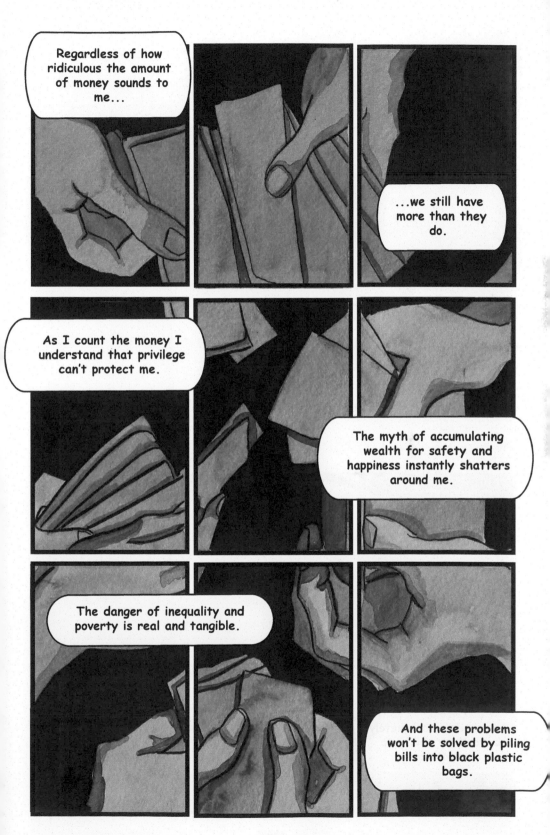

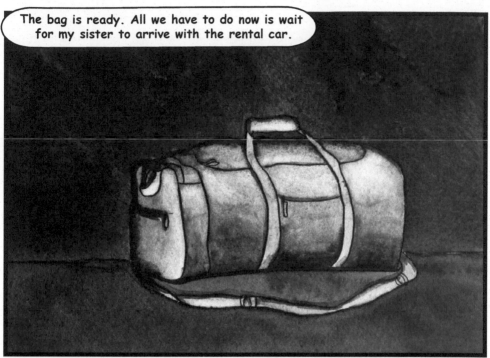

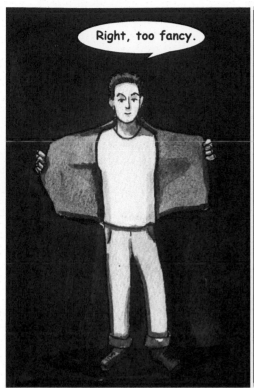

Meanwhile...

...Mario is driving the car my sister rented...

...with the money...

The kidnappers have given us an address...

...where Mario will find a trashcan.

Mario is supposed to leave the money in the trash can...

...and wait a couple of blocks away for further instructions.

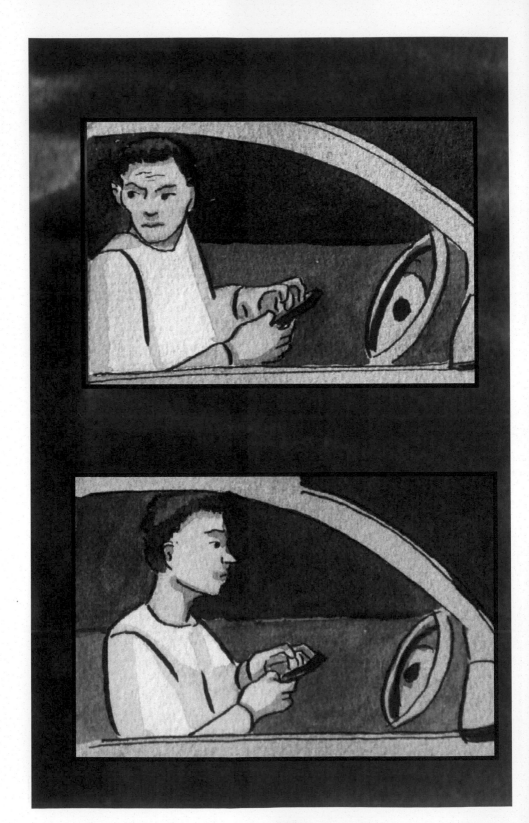

So, he waits.

Nervously.

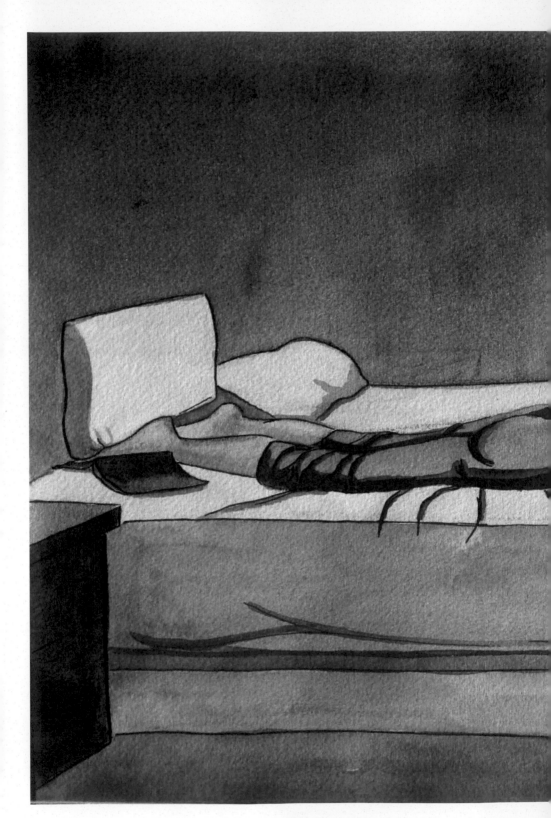

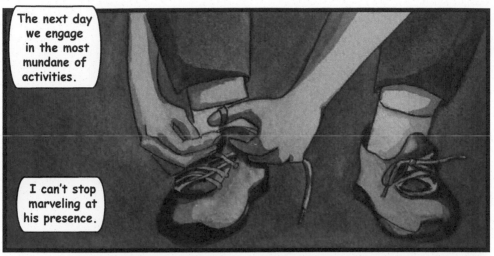

The next day we engage in the most mundane of activities.

I can't stop marveling at his presence.

It's unbelievable to simply look at him again.

A luxury and a pleasure I thought I'd never have again.

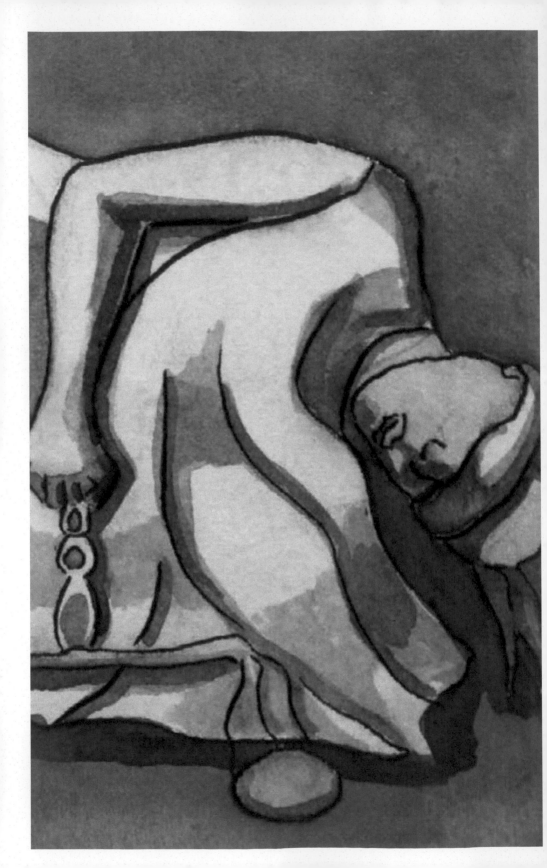

CHAPTER 5

The Aftermath

We have effectively lost our sense of safety so our advisor gives us a "How To Be Safe" talk.

There are a couple of practices that can make you safer.

First of all try to not be predictable. Change your routine up every so often and do not take the same route to and from work.

You are trying to make yourself a more difficult target than the person next to you.

You want to make yourself less attractive to a criminal.

Even if it seems ridiculous or paranoid.

In Mexico or anywhere else in the world, if anyone asks you for your wallet...

...give it to them. Nothing is worth risking yourself for.

Most importantly, if

a kidnapping

were to happen to your family again

you need to keep calm

not negotiate for yourself

and trust, know in your heart,

that your family is doing everything in their power to free you.

Because the truth is...

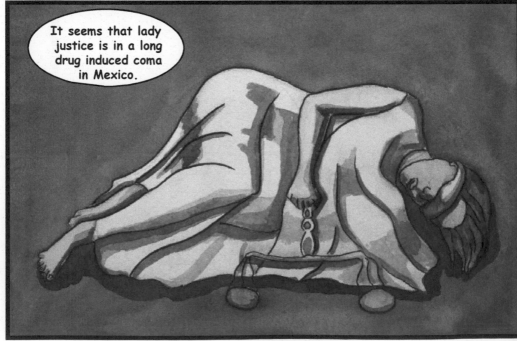

For my parents, there's no choice. They have to move. Not just searching for a safe place to call home but also for a kinder place to heal.

Back home in the USA.

My family is safe but I still feel a lot of fear and paranoia.

The feeling is a sticky black cloud I can't shake off.

It won't let me sleep or feel the safety of home.

I can't feel joy. Jokes are not funny. Life feels dull.

I can't even feel the pleasing warmth of sunshine.

Worst of all, I'm worried for my family in a way I have never been before. It's a current of anxiety beneath the surface which makes me restless.

At home, I feel nothing except worry and numbness. It's a contrast to the adrenaline and emotional intensity I had experienced in Mexico. The world is a dreary and tasteless gray.

The more we shared our story, the more common it seemed to be.

Yeah, we had to move rather quickly because, well... a member of my family was kidnapped.

Oh, Lalo was kidnapped in Mexico too. Right kid?

Yeah. It was a case of mistaken identity they said.

158

But listen to this little one. Apparently some guy showed up at the market where your aunt shops asking for money.

And why exactly should we pay you?

For protection.

Protection from whom exactly?

Me, of course.

Have it by next week. I will come by at 10:00 am. You don't want to know what happens if you don't pay.

This is nonsense. I don't have money to pay.

I agree. I have been pushed far enough.

I say we fight back. I have children to put through school.

My profits have been suffering I don't have the money to pay.

Before we left Mexico and our kind advisor, I had a talk with him. I asked him how I was supposed to go back to normal life.

Please do come in.

You are right, life will never be the same again. You and all of your family have been changed. That is a fact.

But how this changes you is your choice.

You can learn from this, grow, appreciate the time you have with each other and the gift that life is. Or let this experience ruin you, break apart your family and define who you become.

I have seen many families fall apart after an ordeal like this. So I promise you, what happens now is up to you.

Epilogue

LOS SUPERMACHOS

LOS SECUESTROS

¡POR FIN TODA LA VERDAD!

AÑO X – ENERO 31 DE 1974 – REVISTA SEMANAL

Nº 422

$2.00

More Than Money: An Afterword

Sam Cannon

When I turned the last page of *More Than Money* I began to think of the other comics in my collection. I read crime comics, I teach them, I travel long distances just to get them, but the crime stories I had read before were nothing like this book. They were full of gruff one-eyed detectives or masked vigilantes, and these are precisely the types of characters that are not to be found in Claudia Dominguez's story. In the case of her father's kidnapping, there was no Denzel Washington-like hero to tear through Mexico City like in the movie *Man On Fire*, nor was there a charismatic vigilante like Daniel Muñoz and Alberto Maldonado's Pantera to use his martial arts skills to defeat the criminals and seduce the ladies; there was simply a family. In my collection I couldn't seem to find any other crime story like Claudia's. All my crime comics and graphic novels and even movies couldn't manage to tell a story, a true story, like the one I had just read. They didn't even come close. Claudia's story is deep and unsettling, so in an attempt to find something that might resonate with her experience, I left my crime comics and went to one of the Mexican classics: Eduardo Humberto del Río García or Rius.

In 1974 Rius, arguably Mexico's most recognizable comic artist, dedicated an entire issue of *Los Supermachos* to the history of kidnappings in Latin America. Rius carried out extensive research in order to chronicle the development of politically and economically motivated kidnappings in Mexico and across Latin America, but his proposed solution to the horrifying phenomenon was never embraced: simply stop paying any ransom, ever (22). Claudia Dominguez's *More Than Money* picks up Rius' sequential art history of kidnappings in Mexico some forty years later and serves as an emotive study of why *Los Supermachos'* proposal is impossible to implement. Her graphic memoire illustrates the cost that exchanging a human life for money has on individuals and a society – it is much more than simply money. One thing both Claudia Dominguez and Rius share is the exclamation that appears on the cover of *Los Supermachos* Nº 422, as Calzonzín is carried away he cries out: "Esto no es un secuestro sino una violación" ["This isn't a kidnapping, it's a violation"].

More Than Money is a graphic memoir that serves as an artistic exorcism for the author and as a dramatically visual initiation into the violence, fear, and resilience of surviving the kidnapping of a loved one – the violation of the concepts of safety, family, and peace that we often take for granted. Héctor Domínguez Ruvalcaba, a professor I studied with at the University of Texas, explains in his book *Nación Criminal* that fictional narratives, as opposed to official reports by the government, are the sources that enable us to bring to light and understand the meaning of what is legitimate, what can be tolerated, what is obligatory, and what we should fear when confronted with narratives of crime in Mexico (8). He suggests that fiction in literature, film, and the plastic arts can be read as cultural artifacts that describe the formation of "una hegemonía de los grupos criminales" ["a hegemony of criminal organizations"] (11). *More Than Money* illustrates how this criminal hegemony infiltrates almost every aspect of life in Mexico and in turn how it subtly reshapes lives, families, cultures, and nations - even beyond Mexico's borders. News stories, statistics, and official government reports are not fully capable of communicating the reality of kidnapping. Claudia Dominguez's graphic memoire personally links us to the emotions that contort survivors' worldview, sense of safety, and behaviors. The impact of this experience becomes obvious from the first two-page illustration of *More Than Money*.

The first image of the book seems to contradict our expectations - we encounter the narrator's voice in the first text box and see her being forcibly taken by a monstrous spiraling arm, but by the time our eyes reach the final portion of text we are told that it is not she who is being taken but her father, yet he is nowhere to be found - maybe appropriately so. These opening pages can be viewed as a sort of omen or forewarning of how the text contained in these boxes will play out on a personal level for the narrator. Take the time to follow the flowing hair and the straining arm, let your eyes curve along the vortex created by this page layout, and finally land your eyes on her eyes - at the center of this storm and try to feel this tiny mural. These opening pages condense the emotion of the graphic novel you are about to read and say so much more than the accompanying text can tell you. Don't allow your eyes to simply read the text and gloss over the images. This book sits at the comic nexus of other traditions of Mexican visual art; it is a book of small personal murals and votives (*ex votos*) that should be read first as sequential art. A book of suffering and a book of miracles. *More Than Money* is public, it is a mural in book form to be shared with the world and to inform the masses, and yet it is extremely personal like the small votive offerings that briefly recount miraculous occurrences and give thanks for unbelievable outcomes.

As I experienced Claudia's book I felt that it interacted with my sensibilities more on the level of a sequential watercolor mural than a traditional comic book or graphic novel. The opening two-page spread felt more like standing before the harrowing and inspiring murals of David Alfaro Siqueiros or José Clemente Orozco than opening a comic book. Like the Muralists, she illustrates both a broad image of the suffering of the Mexican people as well as their strength and resilience. A swirling painting of a frightened individual gripped by the disembodied arm of violent impunity immediately places this book in communion with the Muralists' depictions of the oppression of Mexico's working classes, and Claudia Dominguez's graphic memoire continues to explore the contemporary reality of criminal hegemony in Mexico: it grips all classes and all sectors of society. The impunity of violence and crime bring us all low.

Claudia explains that Mexico functions on a class system that struggles between what she identifies as the victim class and the criminal classes. She writes, "Everyone in Mexico knows organized crime is an alliance between criminals, police officers and politicians. In a country with rampant poverty it can seem like a better choice to join organized crime, and make some money, than worry about becoming their next victim" (6-7). Her illustration of this reality is even more powerful; it echoes traditional class struggle imagery with the emaciated masses barely able to hold up the weight of the illustration of a police officer, a criminal, and a politician lazily enjoying the spoils of their violent crimes and plotting their next. But it is not only the poorest working class Mexican's that suffer under the weight of the criminals, even Claudia's privileged family finds itself targeted by the criminal classes in their attempt to exploit any group they see as below themselves in the corrupt hierarchy of accumulation. This book's critique of police and political corruption in Mexico is developed within the interior spaces of family life, showing how political violence and crime can reshape our homes and our most intimate relationships.

Claudia's choice to recount her story in the form of a graphic memoire made perfect sense to me as I moved through the illustrations of her memories. Through her craft she is able to introduce us to her family, the spaces they inhabit, the city, and then to the anxiety of waiting and of the unknown. Comics function as a union of image and text and *More Than Money* places these two complimentary parts of the medium of sequential art into sharp juxtaposition. The soft edges of Claudia's watercolor illustrations seem to be violently cut by the stark corners and bold lines of the text boxes and word balloons. The text boxes seem to hover above the rest of the book, signaling the difficulty of narrating the story of her father's abduction. The necessary emotional divorce of the text from the image provides a type of distance between the two that can be felt as a relief from both the intensity of the narration and the emotion of the illustrations. The digital reproduction of the textual narrative and the expressionism of the art can at times appear at odds, but it is precisely this visual tension that mirrors the challenge of re-telling and artistically showing the experience of kidnapping.

Although it may not look like it, *More Than Money* is a crime comic that cuts to the heart of why we want to investigate and solve crimes – it focuses on individuals and how crime and injustice impact us directly. In these cases, there is no justice to be found. Claudia closes her graphic memoire by explaining how she has attempted to recover and how her perception of others, Mexico, and the world has changed. Maybe, this book shares one thing in common with the other crime fiction on my shelves: it is not content with allowing a crime to happen without finding a way for it to teach us something. While the news and politicians argue about crime statistics, Claudia Dominguez's book reveals the reality these headlines have on the lives of a family through sequential art. This graphic memoire is part of a tradition of art, literature, film, and comics that shows us a truth that is often obscured by political discourse. From Rius and *Los Supermachos*, to Mexican crime authors like Paco Ignacio Taibo II or BEF, Claudia tells a story that connects us to one another and exposes our humanity when confronted by the callous impunity of the hegemony of criminal organizations. These stories also teach us about why and how to confront, challenge, and change this criminal hegemony. After considering it, *More Than Money* takes a place among my other crime comics as a unique example of how a gifted artist can tell the missing part of a larger cultural narrative. This book raises a voice and paints a picture (or better yet, multiple pictures) about the personal experience of kidnapping and how this crime, so prevalent in Mexico and across Latin America, is more than a statistic, it is more than money, it is life, it is family.

More Than Money: The Interview

On July 6, 2017 the author and artist **Claudia Dominguez** and **Sam Cannon** held an interview to discuss the process of creating the graphic memoire *More Than Money* and to have a conversation about comics, kidnappings, crime, privilege, immigration, and how to talk about and challenge the systems of inequality that seem to produce criminal impunity like the crime around which Claudia's book revolves.

Sam Cannon: Just to inform everyone, have you published books or graphic novels before? What type of art have you been making up to now?

Claudia Dominguez: I haven't published anything. This is my first one. Yeah, so that's really exciting. I was working, teaching at a university in South Carolina doing mostly gallery work. Just kind of fine arts and fiber arts, like that. It was in that experience that I felt like I was constantly put in a box. I was constantly the token Mexican. That made me want to tell a more detailed story. So that's how I arrived at the graphic novel, because I wanted to be able to tell the story in my own words so people wouldn't just put me in a box, and I also wanted it to be longer than one image.

SC: This book is breaking a whole lot of stereotypes of what people would expect. I'm really excited for your story because it is very different from the narratives you commonly hear about a kidnapping and the hero that saves them, the vigilante that goes after them. It also differs from the Hollywood narratives we've seen like Man on Fire or films like that. Was there any background that you'd like to tell us about that you think would be useful?

CD: I was doing this interview for another project with a girl that's doing the history of Latino surfers. It was really interesting because I felt like I needed to make clear that I grew up as a middle-class Mexican. You know? And that changed a lot of assumptions. A lot of people have the stereotype of the poor Mexican that comes here and doesn't really have any choices and is not educated and is not really a worldly person, etc. etc. I think my situation in general is that I had a great education. I moved here when I was nineteen and I've always spoken English like this. I mean, my parents really put a lot of effort into that. I've travelled a lot and studied a lot and so I think that puts a different spin on it. Sometimes I feel like an imposter, that everyone wants to play the Mexican experience on me, and I'm not really a traditional Mexican in that sense. So, I think it's important to know how classist we are and how I fit in that.

SC: So what part of Mexico is your family from?

CD: So, my mom is from the Gulf of Mexico, from Tampico. My dad is from Mexico City like straight up DF. But I grew up in the State of Mexico in Satélite.

SC: *Yeah, I've driven through there. I lived in Cuautitlán Izcalli so I'm very familiar with that middle class Mexican identity that you don't really see here in the US. So I have maybe a more diverse idea of what being from Mexico can mean. I'm here in Texas and a lot of people are from Northern Mexico and so there is a good understanding of that identity but when it comes to Central or Southern Mexican identities, cultures, and classes it's something a lot of people aren't familiar with.*

CD: Right, it was such a strange experience for me. Now I know it was different, but I always went to really fancy schools with a bunch of Americans where everything was in English. So, I remember in my first year of college and even in high school a lot of my friends had bodyguards. And I was like how awkward is it gonna be that you go on a date? You don't even think about it. You just think about, how are you gonna get laid with that? You know, so I think that shows that I had a non-traditional... or what Americans may think of as a traditional Mexican experience wasn't really mine.

SC: *I think your work is important because it shows that this is still very much a completely valid Mexican experience and that it is at the same time not at all what North Americans would think of as a stereotypical Mexican experience.*

CD: Exactly, because that's very small. Like a stereotype by definition is small, a short-hand for something, a mindless summary, right?

SC: *I think that's really interesting, especially when you talk about the transitions that you went through in this process of seeing how money works, how safety works, and how the feeling of your place in society and culture changed through this experience. I was so interested to see that middle class identity or safety was broken. And I think that's something, in a way, that's relatable for US readers because that's where they live, a lot of them live in that middle-class safety where these things don't touch them, and money means you're fine and your neighborhood means you're fine, you know, etc.*

CD: Definitely. That accumulation of safety doesn't really check with me anymore. I love that this book relates to middle class America because I kept thinking of them as my audience. I kept thinking of making it emotionally real for me and my sister. I thought of my sister as this reader who would help me keep it honest. But I thought of middle class America as the audience; the people that I needed to explain things that maybe were obvious to me, but I wanted them to get it, so they could get the conclusions.

SC: I was looking at your website and you had this one little phrase that said, "When politics become difficult, draw a comic strip." So, I was wondering if you could talk about how that works for you? About how comics can clarify or simplify an issue.

CD: Art for me has always been a way to sort of dig into something deeply. To be able to research it, to study it, and then sort of transfer it - find out how I feel about it, and then spit it back out. That's definitely my process. When I don't understand something, I try to get some sort of sequential order in it and make some art about it.

SC: That's great, sequential order!

CD: Yeah, if only we could organize everything into frames!

SC: Well, in a way you have to re-process everything and re-structure and re-tell that experience, right. So maybe that is part of understanding by breaking down and re-structuring it.

CD: I feel like this is something I have to say: making a graphic novel is like pass after pass after pass of the same story. First you write it, then you do another pass to figure out the moments, and then you do another pass to figure out the storytelling. You keep reviewing the same material over and over. And it felt like every time I did that it became less and less painful to me. So, I mean, it was 100% healing for me, and in a way, I came to terms and realized how I felt about things with every pass that came along. So, when I show it to people they are like, Ahh this is horrible! How did this happen to you? And all I can think about is how this is the best project I've ever done. So, there is a contradiction there.

SC: So, I do have a question about what was your process of creating this graphic novel - the process of writing a script, did you do page gridding and breakdowns, or little bosquejos or borradores? How did that work, the actual process of putting the book together?

CD: I have it a lot more clear right now. This is the perfect time for you to ask me this because I'm writing another one, so I have it really clear in my mind right now. So first I need to have the arc of the story. So, I work with my sketchbook like, what is this story about? Where does it start? What's the trouble? How do we fix it? And why would the audience care? Part of the reason why I want to do graphic novels is because for $20 I can put this in peoples' homes, and to me that's incredible. The whole gallery idea of two people seeing it is so depressing to me. So even if I don't make any money out of the books but the fact that they get to go in peoples' homes is a complete victory. So, I'm constantly thinking, Why would the viewer care? How can I make this character engaging for them? Or, is this something that they would be interested in seeing what happens? Right, so I first deal with that arc: why would anybody care? And after that I start creating moments, individual moments of how the story would go and how those moments would serve me. So, I have a pile of cards, which is what I have for my next book, a pile of cards with moments: Claudia is gonna get on the bus, this matters because it develops the character, and whatever... this leads to something else. So, I have that moment. After that I make little thumbnails, they are really bad and quick, but I make little thumbnails. They are super doodley and crazy and with that I'm trying to figure out, what kind of angle do I want? What kind of character do I want in there? Which angle am I looking at? Which images need to be there? And, how do I express that? Then I go into thinking about the pace of the story. I space it out. Do I tell this quickly? So, I'm getting out of bed and running down the stairs, that's like two quick moments, but when the *chancla* is gonna hit me, I slow it down. So, I'm thinking what I put into a page, the pace. Do I want the viewer to turn a page and see that? Do I want to slow it down? Do I want them to look at that longer? So, how do I do that? So, I have the *chancla* in the face! It's so much fun! Then I go to pencil them, and I kind of pencil just what I want. I make a stick figure, so I can figure out perspective and where things go. Once I have that I look for reference; I either take some pictures or look online and then I can pencil them. There's a lot of preparation!

SC: So, once you have your pacing, your page layouts, that sort of thing done - you do your sketching and pencil work, and then on top of this you do the watercolor?

CD: So, I'll take a pencil drawing and then ink it, then I erase all the pencil drawings and put watercolor on top.

SC: So, it's multiple layers of work on this same page that you've been looking at?

CD: Right! It teaches you courage!

SC: For this project, your book More Than Money, *were any of these illustrations independent paintings that later got put into the story or did you have the whole story ready and then you started creating the images?*

CD: I had the whole story ready and then I started creating the images. I need story to then create images, you know. Everything needs to serve the story. The story for me is number one and number ten. If it doesn't fit the story I don't care for it.

SC: *When I was looking at what you chose to illustrate and to show and the spaces - I mean, when you are making a comic and you are looking at these panels and frames, you as the artist get to choose everything that fits in there. And you can eliminate, you can subtract, you can zoom in or zoom out, and that's really wonderful. And I noticed that a lot of your panels and entire pages spent a lot of time on the atmosphere and the environment rather than on sequences of actions. What was your process... or why were you choosing to show a lot of atmosphere or environment and maybe less action?*

CD: You know when I started this story I thought it was going to be a ten-page story. So, I thought it was going to be a lot shorter and I was going to tell it really factually and I was just going to get it off my chest and I was going to move on. And then I showed it to people and you wouldn't care for the characters. And I think the most important part was because you didn't care for the characters and you didn't feel the helplessness. I really wanted to pace it so that little happens, and you are just kind of waiting for that to happen. So, it turned out that sort of focusing on the atmosphere and the environment was a great way to slow it down and really make the viewer feel the helplessness.

SC: *I really like the pages where you are showing your father with the different jerseys for the soccer teams. That seemed like such a dad moment, that it seemed like this was almost everybody's dad who had something like that. I do think you communicated that process of capturing people and situations.*

CD: I wanted you to care for my dad, and so I wanted to present him as if he could have been anyone's dad.

SC: *So, for you growing up, or as an adult, I was wondering what your relationship with comics and graphic novels has been. And if there were any comics that have impacted your or inspired you to use comic books to tell your stories?*

CD: I've been thinking about that, I can remember when I was fourteen, I have like moments that I remember of comics. So, when I was growing up I loved comics! And I would go and read *X-Men* and whatever, but I would get scolded at home for reading comics because that was a boy thing. It's definitely a bit of a rebellious act to say, I can do this too! Because I don't remember any women authors or there were never any women that truly looked like me, or that remotely didn't look like a doll. So, there's a little bit of a memory about how much I loved comics but that I couldn't fully participate. Then I also remember the devaluation of the peso in 1994 and I remember going to the comic store and instead of buying ten comics I could only buy two or three. And I remember going home and being like, Dad, what the hell? I need more money! This isn't working! And so, my dad gave me this whole political history of what's happening and how our countries are related and blah, blah, blah. And it really made me look at comics like, wow, there are people on the other side of the world making these characters and I'm reading them here. So, there was that power that I found in comic books. But then I kind of disregarded them until adulthood when I started reading some of the more political comics like *Persepolis* or *Maus*. Those are the ones that really inspired me. When I started writing this comic I felt like I just couldn't draw. Like now I feel like I have control of the frame, control of my characters, and the perspective, and I can move them. But when I started I just felt like I couldn't draw but my experience with graphic novels was that they are basically all over the place. You can do anything, like it's not one of those mediums that is very... I don't know, like there's no right or wrong. People have done all kinds of crazy things. There's super experimental ones where you can barely even read and follow, and it just seems like such an open medium that I could just do what came naturally to me and that it would be okay.

SC: I have a question about watercolor. Why choose watercolor? I mean, its not something that you see in a whole lot of comics, especially one about someone getting kidnapped in Mexico City.

CD: You know, when I think of Mexico I think of colors. So, it needed to have color. Many people along the way said, this needs to be ink and that's it, just black and white. And that just never rang true to me. It never felt like that was a way I could tell the story and tell mood. And since not a lot was going to be happening I wanted the color to carry you through. So color was a really important part of the comic for me, even though it's not a very common choice. But I went to Comic Fest in San Diego and a lot of people that are making graphic novels... everybody is making graphic novels with color. So maybe not by-hand painting but it seems like it's a choice that we are all arriving to. So, I think color is going to become the next norm.

SC: I think that there is almost, within the world of graphic novels, the idea that if you want to tell a serious story that it needs to be black and white, just ink.

CD: Yeah, it has to be black and white, and like, I don't know, Mike Mignola style, or has to be whatever style. And that's another beauty of the medium, like I could do whatever I wanted, and I haven't felt that with any of the other art I've made. Graphic novels are so all over the place that it doesn't even matter, just make a choice and go with it. That's exciting to me, and I also love repetition so that helps.

SC: I'd like to get into some of the art, specifically there were some places, like on the first pages of the graphic novel and later on where you paint these big arms. I was wondering, why the giant bodiless arms? What do they mean? How do they work for you visually?

CD: I thought about that a lot, and that is one of the advantages of spending so much time on a project. You get to really think about everything, and I had a really hard time depicting evil. You always see the bad guys are like deformed or ugly or something, and there was no depiction of evil that satisfied that image without it being a stereotype. So, if I'm trying to make a graphic novel about changing peoples' views of what the Mexican experience is, I would just ruin it by having some guy with a moustache and a cigar be the bad guy, right. So, I didn't want to touch any of those stereotypes to begin with, and then the other part is that I was so afraid because I couldn't see them. I didn't know who they were, and they just existed in this random place that I can't even really picture. I think that I wanted the viewer to share the *unknownness* of it, not knowing who they were, where they come from, what they look like or what they're doing. So, I felt like that would make it more powerful, sort of an evil that is unknown rather than an image that I'm providing for you.

SC: Throughout the graphic novel you have illustrations of a lot of landmarks in Mexico City. So, with those different places, one thing I noticed was— well, this is kind of an obsession of mine in my own writing about comics—that I tend to look at landmarks and historic sites, monuments, and illustrations of city spaces. And in your work, one of things about those monuments, with maybe the exception of one panel, is that you show these locations without people in them. We see just the landmarks with no people around. What's going on there? Can you tell me about that?

CD: I didn't even notice that until you brought it up! That completely escaped me and then when you brought it up I realized that it's this memory that you carry with you. Even now that I am terrified of Mexico, you carry this memory of Mexico and when you're homesick you just shine it. Think of it as this token that you carry around in your memories and when you get homesick or you miss it you just embellish it even a little more and with the years it becomes more and more unrealistic and more and more whatever it is that you want it to be. So, I think those images are an expression of the Mexico that is just for me. It doesn't even exist, but I have those monuments that just serve me.

SC: Well, I was wondering because your story talks about crime and about people being kidnapped, people being disappeared, and we have these cities and these places, but these crimes are just taking people out of them. It's like your arm, it just swoops in and grabs people up and they are gone. So, I wonder if you saw anything behind that, just that the people go missing?

CD: You know, I wish I could say yes, but I think if you want to go there that it's more that it took me forever to not be terrified of Mexicans and so now it's like I see Mexicans or I'm surrounded by Mexicans, and I'm like, oh my goodness, anyone of these people could be my father's kidnappers. I think putting them in this shiny memory would have ruined them for me. It's my own mistrust of the people why I didn't put them in there.

SC: In your book you have these moments where you showed those zoomed-out images of the city, those places that you remember, and you have these zoom-ins of these almost archetypal individuals when you talk about the randomness and the life of Mexico City. You have images of the guy with his cart selling paletas and the different people. I thought it was interesting that you went from where you could have shown a crowd you went to showing very specific individuals that we can kind of all recognize. I mean, if you've been in Mexico City you've seen that person even if it's not that exact same person it's like that person still. How was the process of selecting those people to show?

CD: You know, I think at that point I talk a lot about the experience of traveling to Mexico City and one of my favorite things about... oh my goodness, I forgot this word... *transporte público* is that you have to talk to everyone, and everybody's in it. So, interactions in the public system, in the transit system are wonderful to me and they were very enriching to me when I lived in Mexico. So, I wanted to sort of share how we encounter each other, and you know, Mexicans are super perky so why not put them all in there? It's interesting because my next graphic novel is all about how this little girl finds herself through the public transport system.

SC: I remember last time I was in Mexico City I was trying to get somewhere, and I wasn't paying enough attention to subway lines on the map and there was one line that actually wasn't there yet. I think it had an asterisk that said, will be completed in two years or something like that.

And I kept trying to get to this line to get somewhere that didn't exist. But it ended up being a real nice experience going to places I never would have gone otherwise.

CD: If I can go back, it is again, my shining memory and I am choosing what I like about Mexico and maybe the crowds and my monuments are not cool but the people, the individual people, in the subway, now those people are my friends. I don't think I can escape the lens of the immigrant because I have those memories that I unrealistically shine. Like, I don't think that's something I can get rid of.

SC: So, maybe thinking about that concept of those memories and those things that you retain that are kind of idealized, one of the things that does happen in this graphic novel is that that kind of breaks for you. So, I was wondering how your ideas about privilege, money, safety, and poverty have changed through this process?

CD: That is a big one, isn't it? First of all, you arrive to the US and people put you into this category of Mexican, right? And so, you are supposed to be a minority, you are supposed to not have any privilege at all. That took me a long time to understand. I mean I grew up having maids, I grew up going to really fancy schools, so it took me a while to understand that I was supposed to be a minority and how that equated with the Mexicans that were around me too. So, growing up, my dad came from… his father was a carpenter, so they didn't have a lot of money. And so, for him going to school and amassing money was what was going to keep him safe and so hence the high school friends with bodyguards and all that. Like if you belong to that class you're a lot safer than if you don't. That idea, I don't know if I completely believed it in the first place, but after this it's just completely broken. No matter how many bodyguards you have, how much money you have, anyone can be kidnapped, can be attacked in this sense. So, the idea that some are going to accumulate all this money and are going to be safe is just not functional. Before I associated poverty to crime, but if we don't take care of every single citizen then we can't all live there happy. I think that's one of the main things. It made me really look at privilege in a way that I wasn't really comfortable looking at. I had lived in the US for ten or twelve years and I loved pointing out white male privilege, you know, why not? Let's have a party with it! But I grew up with a lot of privilege too and I think that was something that I didn't really want to look at. But when you're putting money in a bag in exchange for your father's life it means nothing to you. You do have to face the fact that you feel this way about money because you have always been comfortable and because you're living a nice life. You know I'm making art and I'm teaching. It's not like I'm hustling or struggling in any real way. So, it made me look at what you have and look at what we do in society.

SC: I really like what you said about making sure everybody is taken care of instead of just thinking about your own little bubble. I think that for me that is one of the things that resonated with the North American experience because I grew up a white male middle class American guy and I lived in this bubble thinking, I'm good so isn't everybody good? I like how your story shows that it can happen in Mexico too and that it can also be popped. Then that experience of getting out of the bubble becomes really important.

CD: Right! Because you're a Mexican in the US and people talk to you and you want to be like, yeah, the struggle. Yes, of course there's a struggle, but I had it really good! To look at that just was not comfortable.

SC: You mentioned that moment of filling the bags with money and making that exchange and the title of your graphic novel is More Than Money *and I found these two moments in your book: one, it's your father's life and that's worth more than money, but also, they took from you more than the money. You didn't just lose X amount of money, you lost a whole lot of other things. So, could you talk about the title and what that means?*

CD: I love that you got that because that's exactly where I was going. The literal sense is definitely that a person is worth to you so much more than money and that's why they can get away with this crime, because you can't put an amount of money for a family member that you love. But then also they take from you so much more than money. The repercussions of that kidnapping were felt by my family for a long time. You know, I don't really know if my dad is still feeling it or how over it he is because he's not going to talk to me about it. But I lost my trust in Mexico, I lost the joy that I had to go down there, I don't even really want to cross the border. All these memories that I had shined completely crumbled. There's a big loss of identity and safety and I don't even live in Mexico City. I mean, Mexico to me it's just this sort of thing that is close to my heart and they took that from me, but just imagine if my dad had to go back to live in the house where you're afraid they are going to come back to get you when they need more money. I wanted to make it clear that yes, this is a kidnapping and yes, we exchanged his life for money, but it is a reign of terror. You know, there are so many people that I talk to in Mexico City that carry two wallets because one is to get robbed and the other one is to buy stuff. There are towns where people aren't really going out after 8pm because you never know what happens. My mom's side of the family in Tampico, they don't really go out unless they have to. They have taken so much from me in one kidnapping and I don't even live there. It's really building so much terror in society that I just don't see a way out of that.

SC: That reminds me of when I lived there, and I mean, I'm a gringo guy and I was driving a lot and so I carried two wallets but to protect me from the police. I would get pulled over all the time because they would see a gringo driving a van and they would be like, "let's see what we can do with that guy." So, I pull out this wallet for the mordida but I have this other one, this other wallet where I kept my other money. So, it's not just necessarily these faceless criminals, it's also... these people who are supposed to protect you.

CD: The police! Right, right! I wanted to express that too, how the police just cannot be trusted. You know, that's something that shocks a lot of Americans, but you cannot call them, you cannot do anything. There is complete mistrust with the police and that is terrifying. Hopefully I got that across too.

SC: I really like the page you have with the police officer and you go through and talk about how he looks and also that he can't be trusted at all. In your book you talked about how you become desensitized to crime and violence especially when something like this hasn't ever affected you. How do you think we can combat that? That acceptance of, well, I'm just not going to go out. Or, it just happens, what are we gonna do about it? Is there something you feel can be done to push against that?

CD: I mean I feel arrogance in it, but I think telling this story is a very powerful medium for that relatability. I thought of my reader generally as a middle class American, but I also thought of my sister as my other audience. I wanted to write this book and sort of remind Mexicans that this is not ok. This is happening way too much. This is really fucked up and we need to realize just how bad this is and do something about it. I have absolutely no idea what we can do about it, but I feel like the telling of our stories and not keeping it quiet is a start. We are creating a vicious cycle of terror, so violence happens and then you don't go outside. So, then it's a lot calmer outside for more violence to happen because nobody's outside. We need everyone to sort of reclaim their lives. We need to just do it, and so if we all did it there would be no way to do crime and then these people would be seen as the outcasts that they are.

SC: Do you think that for you creating this graphic novel is part of that reclaiming your own life?

CD: Absolutely! It definitely made me feel not like a victim. It made me feel like I could do something about it. Especially in a graphic novel that is popular culture that I can put in different places. It has become a medium where I can talk to a lot of activists who are working on this. I met a lady in South Carolina who was making embroidery circles. She was inviting everyone in the community to come out Sundays and embroider the name of a *desaparecido*. And some people were like, what if my son was a bad guy? What if my husband was the bad guy? And they were like, it doesn't matter, we are all in the same boat. It doesn't matter if your *desaparecido* was good or bad just put them in there. Let's just put all that out there. It's also been that communication with other activists that will create a conversation too.

SC: So, there's a series of images and some narrative that kind of explain your thoughts about money and the accumulation of meaningless pieces of paper, is there something that you see as inherently violent about this accumulation of wealth or the drive to accumulate so much money? Does that create violence in our cultures?

CD: Man, I thought about that question and talked about that question with my husband for days. We have created a system that is not equal. So, the accumulation just to have more and to take from others, absolutely. And the obsession we have that says the more you have, the more you're valued or the more you're allowed to do, absolutely. But what if you have a farmer and he's just trying to build something for his family or her family and they're just trying to save a little for the future, a hardworking person. I can't really see anything wrong with that. You know what I mean? So, there's definitely an idea about billionaires, my husband kept telling me that billionaires shouldn't exist, and that's true! We shouldn't have that division of wealth. I don't think anyone should be able to accumulate so much on the back of somebody else. And I feel like such a traitor saying this too.

SC: I mean, in a way we are all kind of locked into that system and contribute to it, but we also want to fight against it and I think we are all in a hard spot. So...

CD: Exactly, I mean I can't with a clear conscience say that the accumulation of wealth is evil when I am enjoying a lot of it. And the fact that I have these thoughts towards money is because I have enjoyed all of it. I agree with that, that we are all in this system and I don't know how we can make it more equitable. Well, I do believe in a universal basic income...

SC: Well, that goes back to your idea that everybody should be taken care of and nobody should be left out. Going back to your previous thought there and I think that visually and artistically in your graphic novel there is this great two-page illustration where at the top half you have the politician, the criminal, and the police and on the bottom, you have all the people literally holding them up on their backs. I thought that image said a whole lot. Can you tell me about it?

CD: Right! I love that image! And that one is actually a really long painting. It's a really large painting that I enjoyed making. It's connected to that reign of terror. I have politicians, drug dealers, and the cops that all live together or operate together. Everybody knows who they are, where they live, what they do, but it doesn't bother them because they think we have absolutely no power. All these excesses that they have hurt everybody else. They make everybody else poor. They make everybody else hurt. They just make a terrible situation for everybody else. I saw this sculpture, it was a knee-high sculpture and it was just kind of a shiny bronze plate on the top and it had a little bit of space where you could see there was something there but you couldn't tell what it was, but then when you looked underneath there were hundreds of little people holding up this giant plate. I mean, I stepped on this sculpture, I walked by the sculpture a million times before I actually saw the people. That was a really powerful moment for me, to look underneath and see all the little people there. That was the initial inspiration for that.

SC: I love that page of your book. I think, kind of connected to this, one thing that is interesting when you get to the end of your graphic novel you start to have these interactions with immigrants in the US. Your narrative isn't the only one. Can you talk a little bit about the narratives of immigrants and undocumented communities in the US that connect to your experience?

CD: When we came back it seemed like everybody we talked to had a story like that. It seemed like every time I talked to a family member they knew of somebody else that this had happened to. So, I thought for Mexicans there is this problem of normalization, that we think it doesn't happen to us, and it's not that big of a deal, but every single Mexican I talk to has somebody that this has happened to. So, I wanted to make the point that it didn't just happen to my father. It's happening all around and it's happening way too much. I also wanted to point out that a lot of us are coming to the US as refugees. We are running away from violence. The only reason you are going to leave your home to come to a place where you are not really appreciated is because home is too dangerous, or home is too scary. So, hustling in the US is a better answer than being home afraid that you're going to get kidnapped again and your family is going to fall apart again, and all of this is going to happen. So, I really wanted to make that point. Any immigrant you find could be running here because their life is in danger.

SC: Yeah, the narrative that is the dominant narrative here is, they're coming for our jobs, and that's not the story that you hear when you actually talk to people one-on-one, individually.

CD: And all those stories in the book are true too.

SC: I thought that was a really interesting way to challenge that discourse that we get here in the US and connect your work to the broader immigrant community. On one side, in Mexico we have this crime that is adversely affecting people and they are trying to escape it as refugees in a way, to get away from it. And now here we have I.C.E. and the government going after these people and snatching them out of the lives they've made here. So, it's happening on both sides, this disappearing, this violent... people being torn out of their lives.

CD: It's so depressing to see just how hostile the US has become to everyone that's not white and male and crazy. It's so heartbreaking, the travel ban for Muslims, all the derogatory talk about women, and Mexicans are obviously caught in the crosshairs. I think it has become worse and more real for me. I have a cousin that was living in Tijuana and he came to visit, and he came over and told me, I live in the fanciest part of Tijuana because I'm really worried about the crime in Tijuana. It just feels like somebody's going to rob you all the time. But even there, there are a lot of, he called them, destitute people. A lot of people that have been deported and they are just homelessly sitting there. A lot of sick people, people basically dying in the street because they've been deported, and they don't have anywhere to go and sometimes they are even thinking of coming back in. So, what do you do? You're home and you're in this violent town and you run to the US and you have that hostility towards you again. So, it just seems like the rich get richer and we heap up even more of our people that don't have the means. There is so much about immigration that is so upsetting, you know, when white people immigrate it is Manifest Destiny, but if you are brown in any way you're told, please get out. I think that's something that I'll have to explore in about 220 pages.

SC: I would love to read that. Yes, yes, do it! I like the tradition in graphic novels of memoir; things like Persepolis or Maus that are graphic memoir. I liked earlier when you talked about memory and emotion and there is more than just action that you can do in comic books. But when I look at your book I also see something of Mexican art. And this is totally my perspective, where I'm coming from, but when I open your book and I see that first two-page spread of the arm wrapping around and holding you, or graphic novel you, I was so much reminded of the first time I walked into the Palacio de Bellas Artes and [Claudia: YES!] saw those murals. This sweeping, the motion of it, the colors, the texture, and the violence of it. Were the Mexican Muralists a source of inspiration for you in doing this project?

CD: Definitely, I look at Mexican art all the time. The Muralists are definitely up there when it comes to expressing. Guadalupe Posada, you know his political art, I love its anarchic criticism for politicians because the political comics in the US just kind of make fun of the politicians. But Guadalupe Posada turns them into pigs, turns them into animals, he really changes the feeling of it by making it so much more surreal. So, I wanted some of that surrealism and that violence to be expressed in the emotional authenticity of the experience. When I was in graduate school in North Carolina, I failed my first-year review. I realized then that my aesthetics were very very Mexican, and I needed to figure out where they were coming from and what they were. So, I could present them in a way that Americans would be able to understand them and weigh in. At that point my aesthetics were very Mexican and were a problem, but I absolutely love them, and not only do I want to stay there, but truth is expressed through surreal color. So that is definitely where I am.

SC: Your graphic novel has so many pages that are large, full-page or two-page spreads, that it's like... if somehow there were Muralist paintings in book form... this would be a graphic mural or a Muralist novel, I don't know what I'd call it, but something along those lines.

CD: Yeah, instead of using little frames I just go for the big picture! I felt that way, I thought, if you have both pages and you open it with an image that goes from the left to the right that it can surround you. You think of the intimacy of reading that book and how you travel through it, it's something that I really like about the medium.

SC: Before we had ever met or had a conversation, when I sat down with your book that's what I thought of, of those murals, of Orozco or Siqueiros. And with that comes their political messages and their ideology, and so this story can continue that. We talked before about the two-page spread with the image of all the masses struggling under the weight of the police and criminals – it's a visual tradition that is very Mexican, of the people, of the Revolution. For me that is something visual that was communicated through your book but that also came through in the narrative, and I appreciated that.

CD: Thank you. That's always been my bind as a Mexican, when you grow up middle class you are always pushed towards things that are abroad: Europe or the US. Don't really be brown, don't stand in the sun. There's all these shoulds that keep us away from Mexican culture. But I always loved the people and the Mexican culture and popular culture and it's something that was never really accepted or valued when I was growing up. But when I got to the US, I realized I could just have it, nobody even knew what was going on and so it didn't even matter. But at the same time, I grew up with all that art and color within my home, but I wasn't really allowed to be part of the people. I always feel this sort of wish that I was but at the same time if I had been I wouldn't have all these opportunities, so that to me is a conundrum, it's a problem that I will explore. That push...

SC: Well, I feel like in your story you talk about, even just now we've talked about, the experience you went through as something that crosses all classes and all groups of people in Mexico – they are all affected by this type of crime, and the politics of it, the organized nature of it. That experience is shared, and in a way levels everyone, right?

CD: So, all of us are the people! Yes! At the end of the day I do believe that! We are all in this together. It doesn't matter how much money you have or how many cars you have—they can attack you just the same. So, yes, I'm so glad you mentioned that. This conversation has made me realize just how much we are all in this together!

SC: Maybe it's like a seesaw, those wealthy guys and the politicians, the police are at the high end, but they are only up there because everybody else is down here on the low end. Hopefully, eventually, we can get the things to get a little more even or flip the other way.

CD: We will eventually!

The Final Word

Pamela Jackson

I met Claudia in 2017 at San Diego Comic Fest, where she was an artist in search of a publisher, passing out sample pages of her graphic novel. I was struck by her enthusiasm for the medium and shaken by her harrowing personal tale.

The stories we tell have the power to help us both transcend and embrace our everyday differences. Our stories make us human and weave together a shared cultural heritage. With growing options for publication—both physical and virtual—and a format with forgiving artistic "rules," the graphic memoir genre has opened up the comics medium to new authors and readers who might not otherwise be avid fans of comics. The format of graphic memoir allows the creator to revisit the past, reimagine trauma, and reclaim their own life's narratives. Memoir creation has a diary-like power that can aid the author in healing from traumatic life experiences. Indeed, in her interview with Sam Cannon, Claudia talks about bringing a "sequential order" to life's challenges and mysteries and how the process of creating a graphic memoir helped her re-balance feelings of victimization.

An author of nonfiction prose myself, I am familiar with the emotional power of memoir writing. As a comics fan, I believe the visual-verbal medium allows readers to develop a deep, empathic connection to the author and his or her characters. In his afterword, Sam Cannon writes, "As I experienced Claudia's book..." *Experienced*. Therein lies the power of sharing illustrated memories. By combining rich visuals with narration, readers can engage with graphic storytelling to more fully experience reflections of the author's pain, passion, struggle and triumph.

Graphic memoir reclaims the author's power while often shining light on systematic oppression and inequality. Stories like Claudia's deserve to be told and need to be collected. In a growing field of library scholarship, Critical Librarianship (critlib), practitioners share a dedication to social justice and a deep concern for human and economic rights. There is a growing movement that believes libraries and librarians have a significant role to play in challenging power and privilege in order to bolster engaged, informed and empowered people. In *More Than Money*, themes of social class, corruption, power and marginalized voices are a perfect fit for collections that aim to engage readers with issues of identity, social justice, human rights, and economic equality. Collecting these graphic narratives, sharing them with readers, and using them in classes are one step toward building a more compassionate global society.

About the Author

Claudia Dominguez was born in Mexico City and moved to the United States at the age of 19. She is an artist and graphic novelist whose work is informed by her native Mexico and her immigration to the United States. She explores political themes—specifically how violence affects society and individuals on both sides of the border. The author is currently working on her next graphic novel. To keep up with her current projects, visit storiesanddrawings.com

Contributors

Frederick Luis Aldama works in the departments of English as well as Spanish and Portuguese, and teaches courses on Latino and Latin American cultural phenomena, including literature, film, TV, music, sports, video games and comic books. He is also an affiliate faculty of the Center for Cognitive and Behavioral Brain Imaging. Aldama is the author, co-author and editor of over thirty books. He is founder and director of the White House Hispanic Bright Spot awarded Latino and Latin American Space for Enrichment Research (LASER) program. He

is founder and co-director of Humanities and Cognitive Sciences High School Summer Institute at The Ohio State University, and has been honored with the 2016 American Association of Hispanics in Higher Education's Outstanding Latino/a Faculty in Higher Education Award.

Sam Cannon is the Bruce and Steve Simon Professor of Language and Literature and Assistant Professor of Spanish at Louisiana State University Shreveport. Professor Cannon teaches undergraduate language and culture courses and graduate seminars on Latin American literature, film, and comics. He received his M.A. in Hispanic American Literature from the University of Arkansas and earned his Ph.D. in Iberian and Latin American

Literatures and Cultures at the University of Texas at Austin. Professor Cannon has developed courses that focus on social justice issues related to colonialism, globalization, and political violence in the context of Latin America, as well as worked with his local communities to promote social causes. His research, presentations, and publications explore representations of economic and political violence in Latin American comics and graphic novels.

Pamela Jackson is the Popular Culture Librarian in Special Collections and University Archives at SDSU. Her research interests include diversity and culture as reflected in comic art and the impact of popular culture collections on teaching and learning. Her works include a grant-funded humanities website, *The Comic-Con Kids: Finding and Defining Fandom*, which explores the emergence of comics, science fiction and fantasy in the youth counterculture movements of the 1970s. Pamela has an MA in English with an emphasis on Creative Writing from Sonoma State University and an MA in Library and Information Studies from the University of Wisconsin at Madison.

William Anthony Nericcio is the director of SDSU Press and the publisher of Amatl Comix. Born in Laredo, Texas, and educated at the University of Texas, Austin, and at Cornell University, he works as the Director of MALAS, the Master of Arts in Liberal Arts and Sciences program. He is the author of *Tex[t]-Mex: Seductive Hallucinations of the "Mexican" in America* with UT Press. His forthcoming book, authored with Frederick Luis Aldama, is *#browntv: The Revolution Will Be Televised,* appearing in 2019 from the Ohio State University Press.